Lerner SPORTS

ALL-STAR SMACK DOWN

TRAVIS KELCE VS. ROB GRONKOWSKI

WHO WOULD WIN?

KELLEY BARTH

Lerner Publications ◆ Minneapolis

The stats and information in this book are accurate through the 2024–2025 season.

Lerner Publications Company
An imprint of Lerner Publishing Group, Inc.
241 First Avenue North
Minneapolis, MN 55401 USA

For reading levels and more information, look up this title at www.lernerbooks.com.

Main body text set in Aptifer Sans LT Pro.
Typeface provided by Linotype AG.

Library of Congress Cataloging-in-Publication Data

Names: Barth, Kelley author
Title: Travis Kelce vs. Rob Gronkowski : who would win? / Kelley Barth.
Other titles: Travis Kelce versus Rob Gronkowski
Description: Minneapolis : Lerner Publications, [2026] | Series: Lerner Sports. All-star smackdown | Includes bibliographical references and index. | Audience: Ages 7–11 | Audience: Grades 2–3 | Summary: "With seven Super Bowls between them, Travis Kelce and Rob Gronkowski are two of the best tight ends in NFL history. Discover their greatest moments and key stats then decide for yourself which is better"—Provided by publisher.
Identifiers: LCCN 2025011522 (print) | LCCN 2025011523 (ebook) | ISBN 9798765689448 lib. bdg. | ISBN 9798348028381 pbk | ISBN 9798765694305 epub
Subjects: LCSH: Football players—United States—Rating of—Juvenile literature | Tight ends (Football)—United States—Statistics—Juvenile literature | Kelce, Travis, 1989- | Gronkowski, Rob, 1989- | Sports rivalries—United States—History—Juvenile literature | LCGFT: Statistics
Classification: LCC GV939.A1 B3685 2026 (print) | LCC GV939.A1 (ebook) | DDC 796.332092/2—dc23/eng/20250606

LC record available at https://lccn.loc.gov/2025011522
LC ebook record available at https://lccn.loc.gov/2025011523

Manufactured in the United States of America
1 – CG – 12/15/25

TABLE OF CONTENTS

Travis Kelce

INTRODUCTION

FOOTBALL LEGENDS

It was February 1, 2015, and the biggest game of the year was about to begin. Tight end Rob Gronkowski and the New England Patriots were facing the Seattle Seahawks in Super Bowl 49. The

 **FAST FACTS** 

- Rob Gronkowski holds the record for the most receiving touchdowns for a tight end in a single season with 17.
- Gronkowski won the Comeback Player of the Year award in 2014 after returning from a knee injury.
- Travis Kelce holds the record for the most receiving yards for a tight end in a single season with 1,416.
- Kelce was the fastest tight end to reach 10,000 receiving yards.

teams were tied 7–7 just before halftime. Patriots quarterback Tom Brady saw an opening and threw a 22-yard pass. Gronkowski caught the pass and stepped into the end zone, bringing the score to 14–7.

Gronkowski caught six passes for a total of 68 yards during the game. His efforts helped the Patriots win 28–24. Gronkowski had just won his first Super Bowl. And it wouldn't be his last.

Five years later, on February 2, 2020, the Kansas City Chiefs were playing the San Francisco 49ers in Super Bowl 54. Tight end Travis Kelce was hoping to lead the Chiefs to their first Super Bowl win in 50 years. But the Chiefs were down 20–10 as the fourth quarter started. They had to score some more points, and fast.

Rob Gronkowski

Kelce knew what to do. He ran to the end zone and was wide open for a pass from quarterback Patrick Mahomes. Kelce's touchdown helped kick off a fourth-quarter comeback for the Chiefs. They won 31–20. Kelce caught six passes for 43 yards. After six seasons in the National Football League (NFL), he had won his first Super Bowl. And just like Gronkowski, he was just getting started.

Travis Kelce and Rob Gronkowski are both all-star tight ends. But who would win in a head-to-head showdown? Let the smackdown begin!

Rob Gronkowski (left) avoids a Seattle Seahawks defender to make a catch in his first Super Bowl appearance.

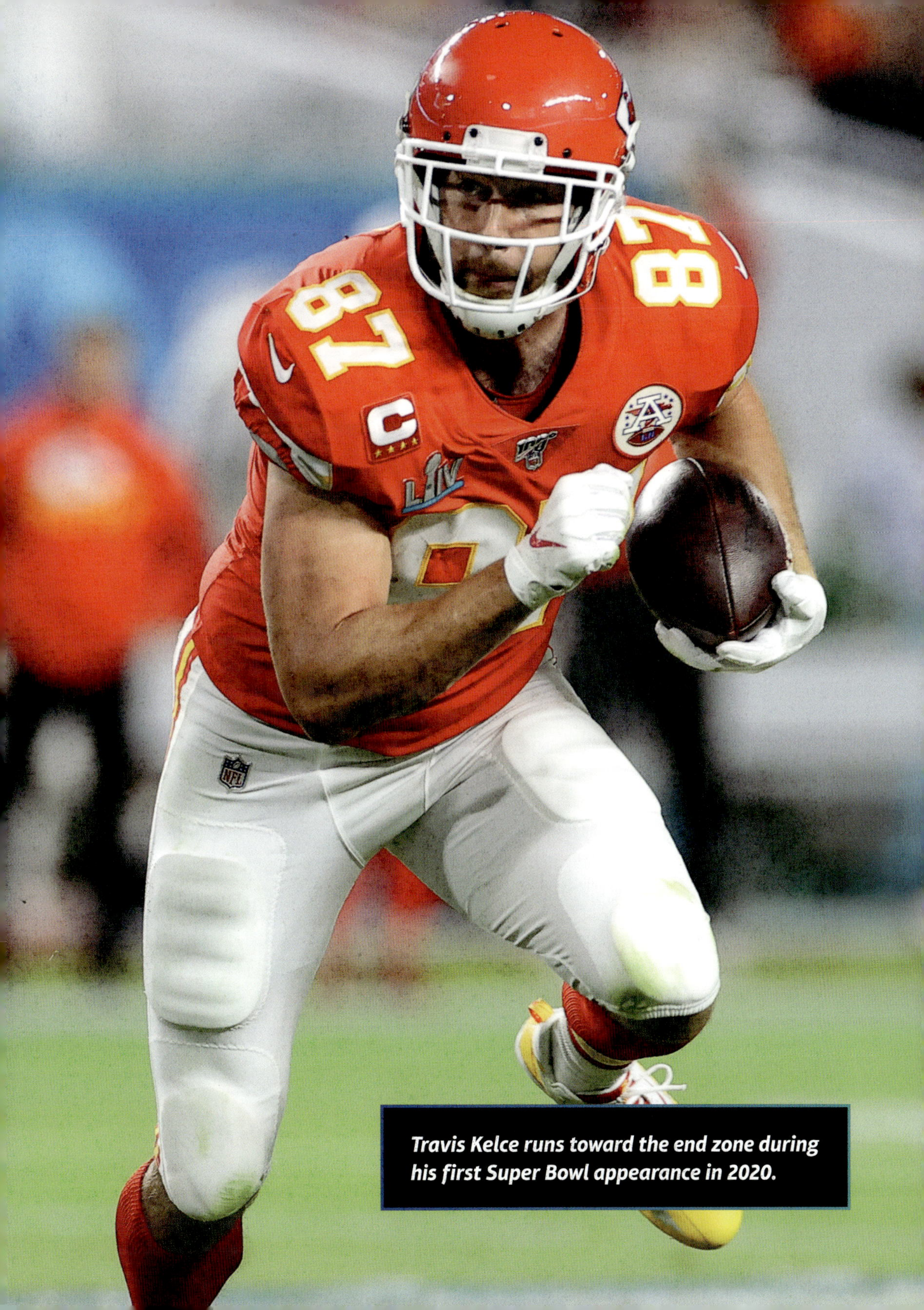

Travis Kelce runs toward the end zone during his first Super Bowl appearance in 2020.

CHAPTER 1

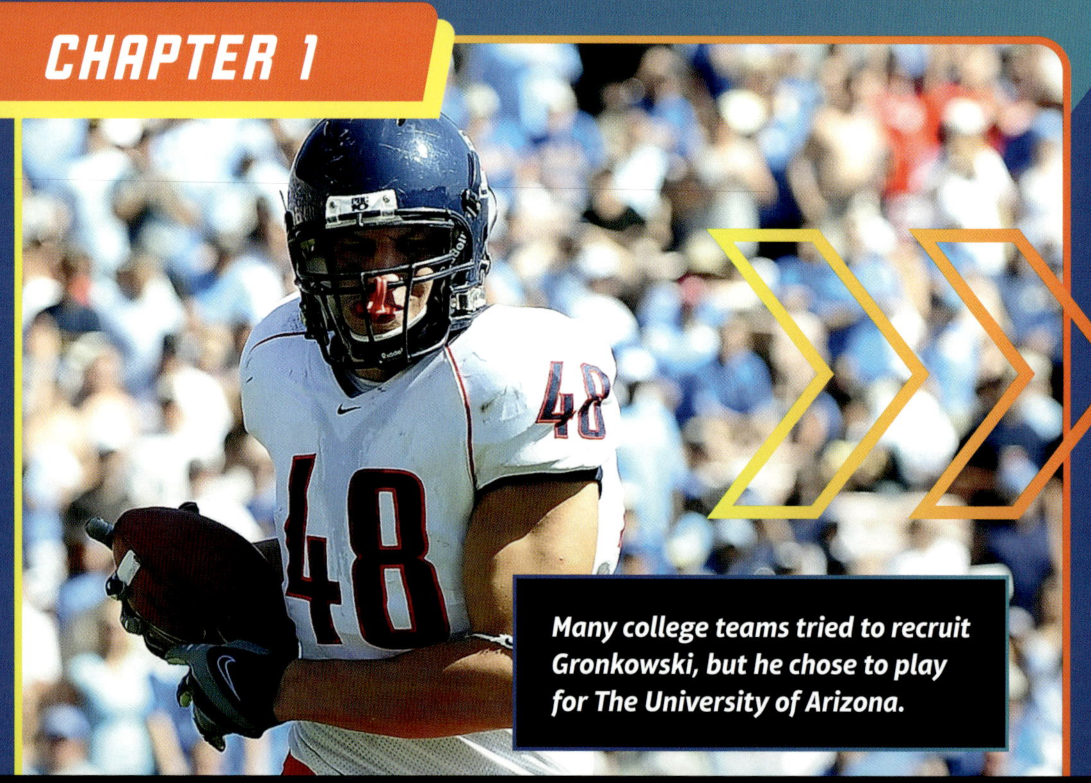

Many college teams tried to recruit Gronkowski, but he chose to play for The University of Arizona.

JOURNEY TO GREATNESS

Rob Gronkowski was born May 14, 1989, in New York. He played multiple sports growing up, including hockey and baseball. In high school, he focused on basketball and football. By his senior year, Gronkowski was an all-state player and one of the best tight ends in the country. Colleges took notice. The University of Arizona recruited him in 2007.

Gronkowski had 28 receptions for 525 total yards during his first year, including six touchdowns. The next year, he played even better. Even after missing the first three games of the season, he had 47 receptions for 672 total yards. He scored 10 touchdowns, the most on his team. Gronkowski broke many University of Arizona records , including most catches, yards, and touchdowns of any tight end in the history of the school.

Gronkowski didn't play his third year of college because of an injury. After recovering from back surgery, he decided to leave college and go pro. The New England Patriots picked him in the second round of the 2010 NFL Draft.

Gronkowski runs in a 51-yard touchdown during a 2007 game for the Arizona Wildcats.

Travis Kelce was born on October 5, 1989, in Ohio. He also played multiple sports growing up, including baseball and basketball. He was the quarterback of his high school football team. But when he went to college at the University of Cincinnati, there were questions about what position he would play.

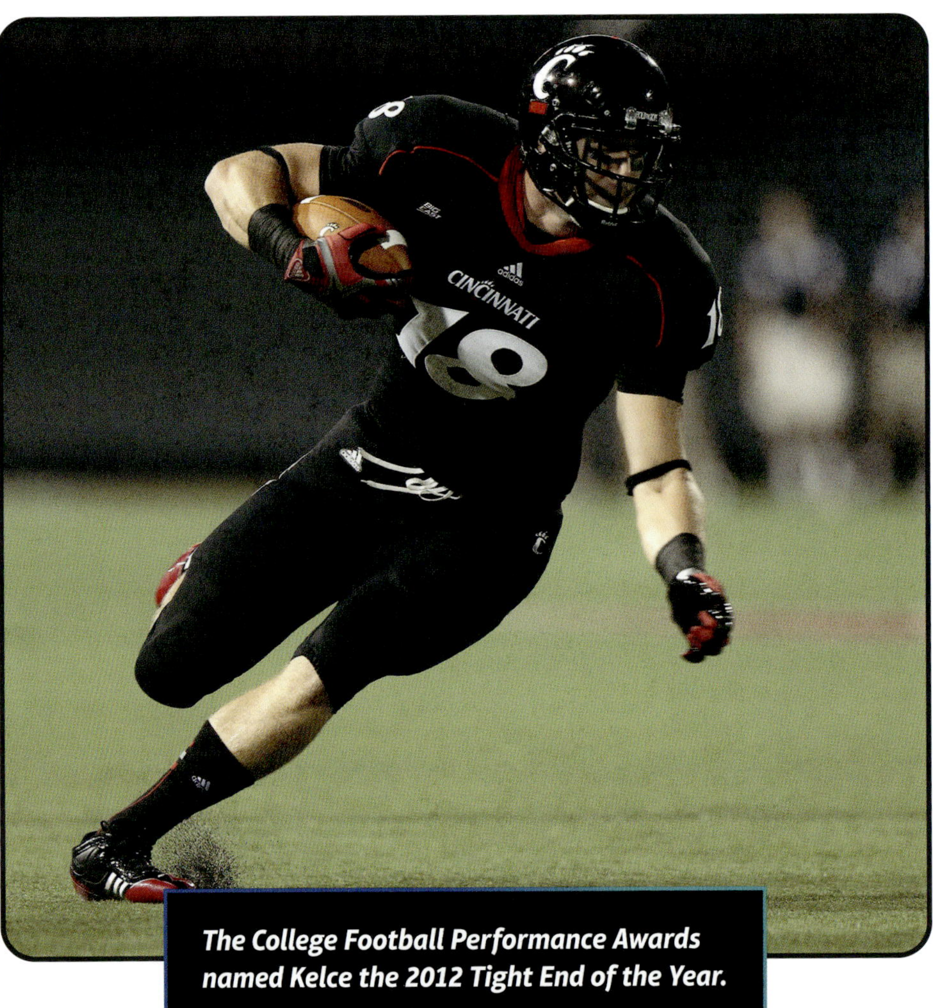

The College Football Performance Awards named Kelce the 2012 Tight End of the Year.

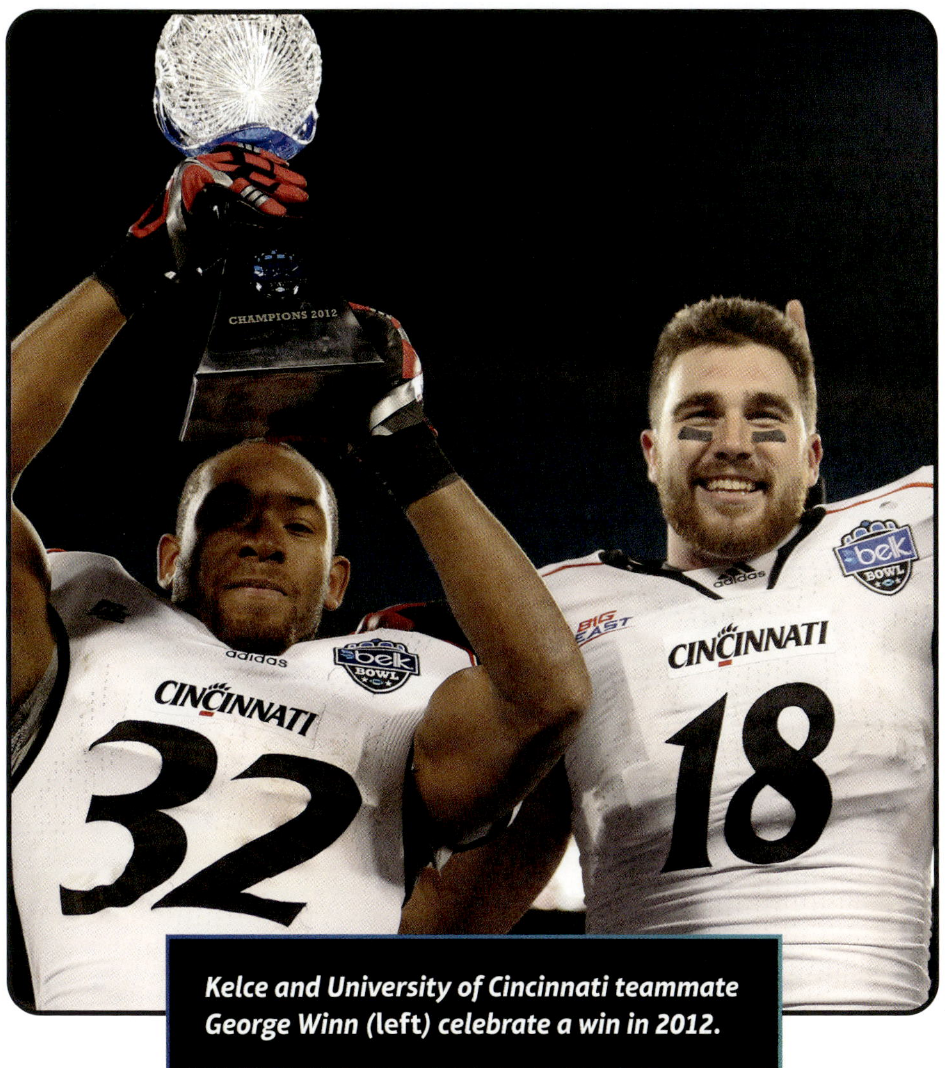

Kelce and University of Cincinnati teammate George Winn (left) celebrate a win in 2012.

Kelce wanted to be a quarterback. But his coach thought he would make a better tight end. Kelce wasn't convinced. But watching Gronkowski play in the NFL helped change his mind. He saw that being a tight end could be fun, so he agreed to switch positions.

The change paid off. During his final college season in 2012, Kelce had 45 catches for 722 total yards. He also scored eight touchdowns. The following year, he was the 63rd overall pick in the NFL Draft by the Kansas City Chiefs.

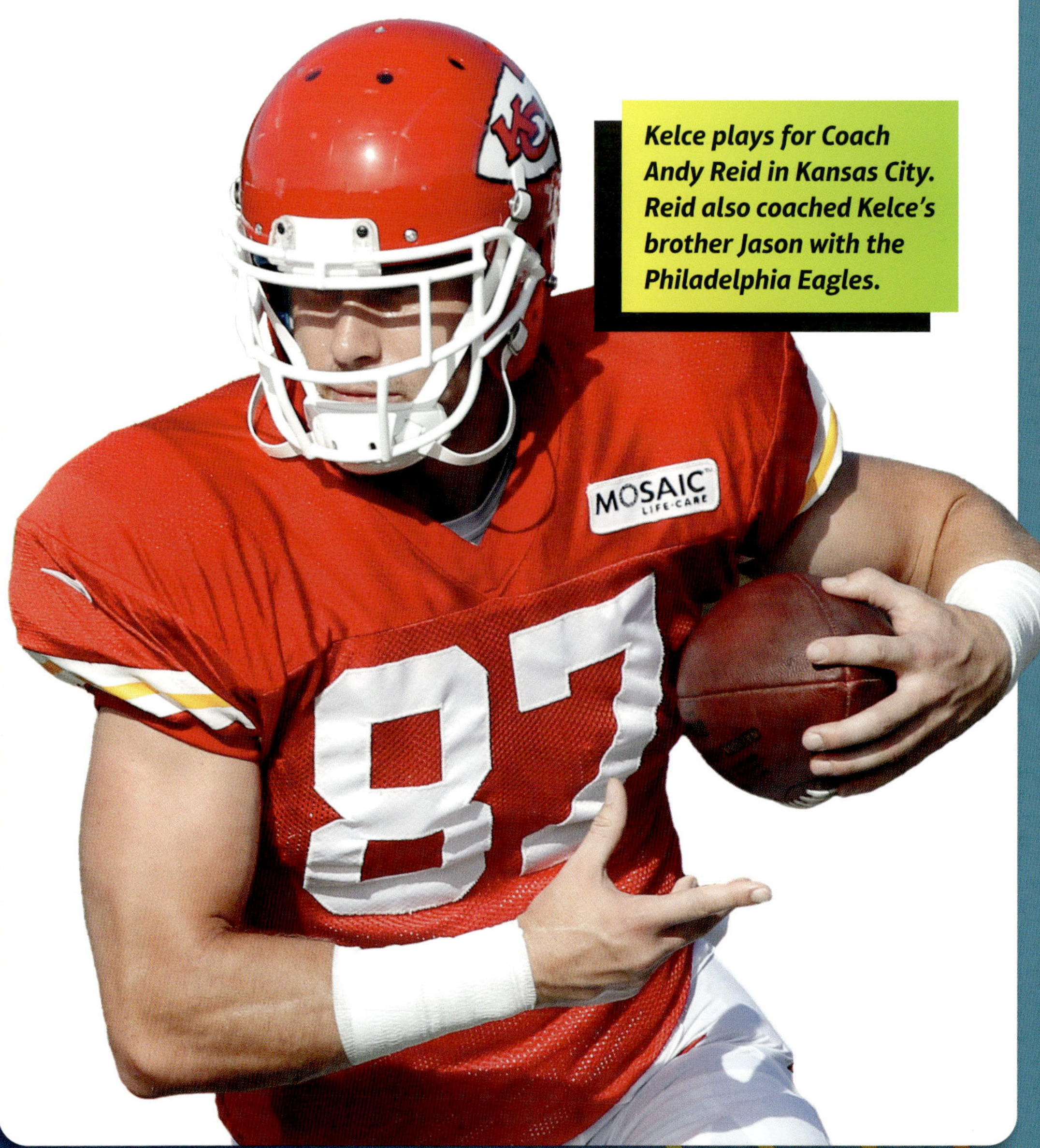

Kelce plays for Coach Andy Reid in Kansas City. Reid also coached Kelce's brother Jason with the Philadelphia Eagles.

Gronkowski and three of his brothers, Gordie Jr., Dan, and Glenn (left to right)

CONSIDER THIS

Gronkowski and Kelce aren't the only sports stars in their families. Gronkowski's brothers Dan, Chris, and Glenn also played in the NFL. Kelce's older brother Jason played with the Philadelphia Eagles for 13 years. In 2023, Jason and Travis became the first brothers to play against each other in a Super Bowl.

CHAPTER 2

Gronkowski wore the number 87 jersey during his nine years with the New England Patriots.

GREAT MOMENTS

Rob Gronkowski got off to a strong start in the NFL. He was a two-time Rookie of the Week winner in 2010. He was also the youngest rookie ever to catch three touchdown passes in one game.

Gronkowski broke several records the next season. He had career highs of 90 receptions for 1,327 yards. He also snagged 17 touchdown catches. This was a new NFL record for touchdowns by a tight end in a single season. In a playoff game against the Denver Broncos, he caught three touchdown passes. With 10 catches and 145 yards, Gronkowski had more catches than every Broncos player combined.

After dealing with injuries, Gronkowski had another great season in 2014. He won the Comeback Player of the Year award that year. He helped lead the Patriots to Super Bowl wins in 2015 and 2017. One of his best Super Bowl performances was in 2018. He grabbed nine receptions for 116 yards and two touchdowns.

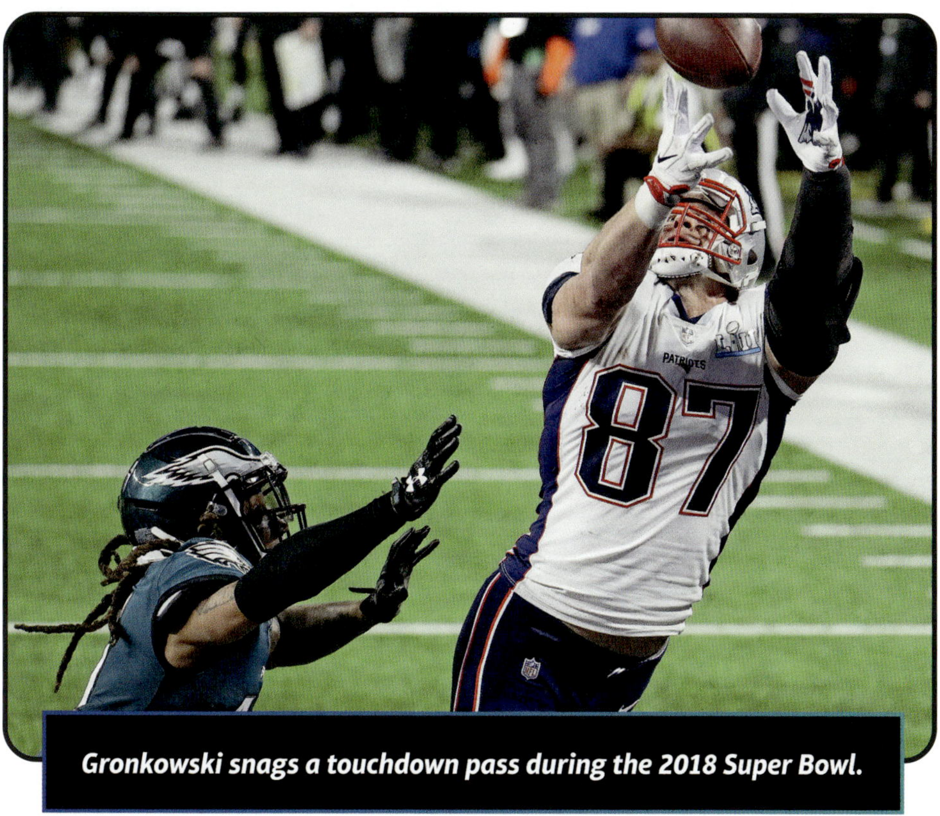

Gronkowski snags a touchdown pass during the 2018 Super Bowl.

Gronkowski and quarterback Tom Brady (right) celebrate their 2021 Super Bowl win after defeating Kelce and the Chiefs.

Gronkowski decided not to play in the 2019 season. Injuries kept him from enjoying the game. He considered retiring for good. But in 2020, he decided to return to the NFL. He joined the Tampa Bay Buccaneers to play with former teammate Tom Brady.

He and Brady won another Super Bowl with the Buccaneers in 2021. In that game, Gronkowski became the first player to ever catch a pass in five different Super Bowls. After this milestone, Gronkowski retired for good at the age of 33.

Travis Kelce's rookie season wasn't a success. He injured his knee and needed surgery before the first game of the season. But by 2016, he was proving himself a successful

CONSIDER THIS

Gronkowski played for 11 years in 165 total NFL games. He has 10,675 receiving yards and scored 107 touchdowns. That is about 65 yards per game. Kelce has played 12 NFL seasons so far for a total of 200 games. He has a total of 14,229 receiving yards, which is about 71 yards per game. He has also scored 97 touchdowns.

tight end. In a regular-season game against the Denver Broncos, Kelce had 11 catches for 160 yards. His most impressive moment was when he caught a short pass and ran for an 80-yard touchdown. He led all tight ends in receiving yards that year.

Kelce runs down the field after catching a pass against the Buffalo Bills.

Kelce warms up before Super Bowl 59 in 2025.

By the 2020 season, Kelce and the Chiefs were headed to their second Super Bowl in two years. He had already had an impressive season with a career-high 1,416 yards. That broke the NFL record for tight ends. Despite his record-breaking season, Kelce and the Chiefs lost in the Super Bowl to Rob Gronkowski and the Tampa Bay Buccaneers.

But Kelce continued to rack up yards and break records. In 2022, he racked up a personal record of 110 catches for a career-high 12 touchdowns. Kelce helped the Chiefs win the Super Bowl two years in a row in 2023 and 2024.

One of Kelce's biggest strengths is his ability to stay healthy. He has only missed five games since his rookie year. Gronkowski, on the other hand, battled many injuries throughout his career. He had to miss large parts of multiple seasons.

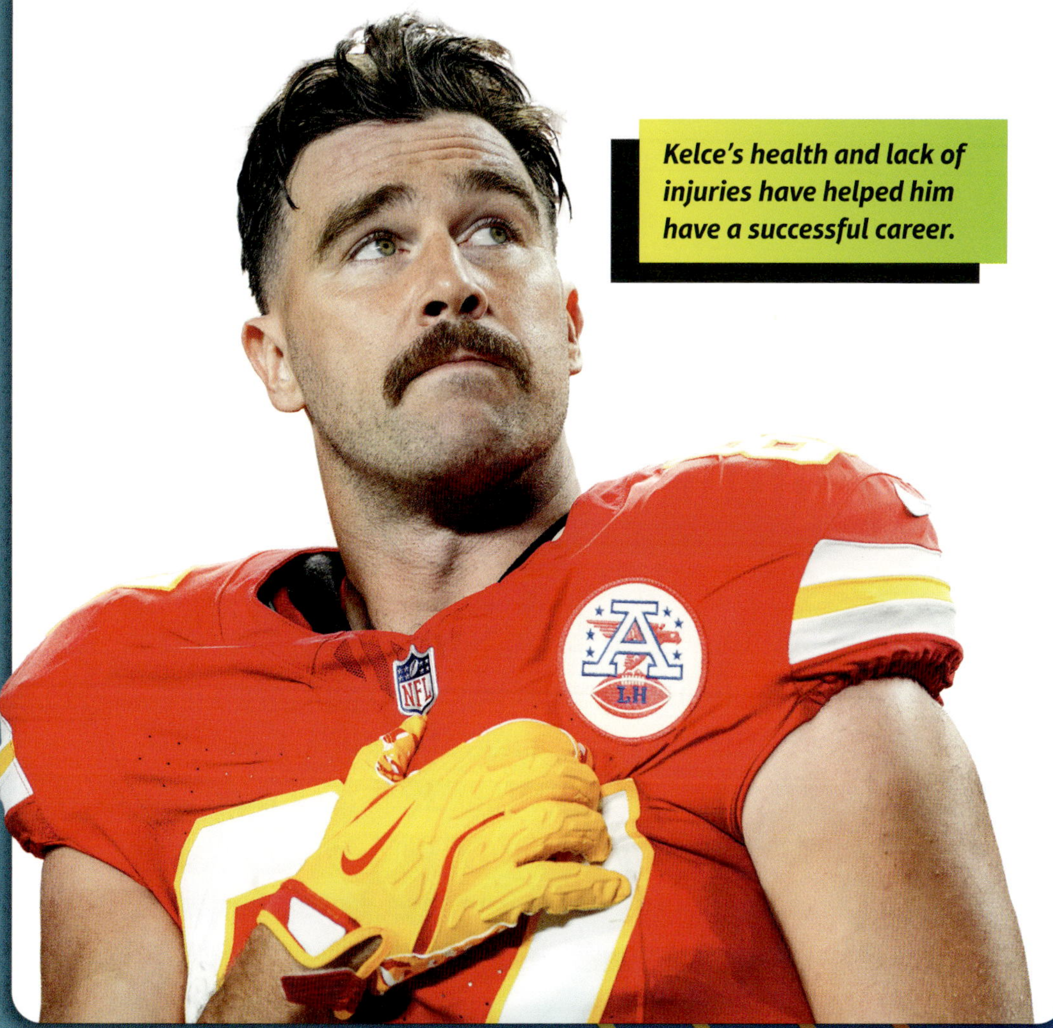

Kelce's health and lack of injuries have helped him have a successful career.

CHAPTER 3

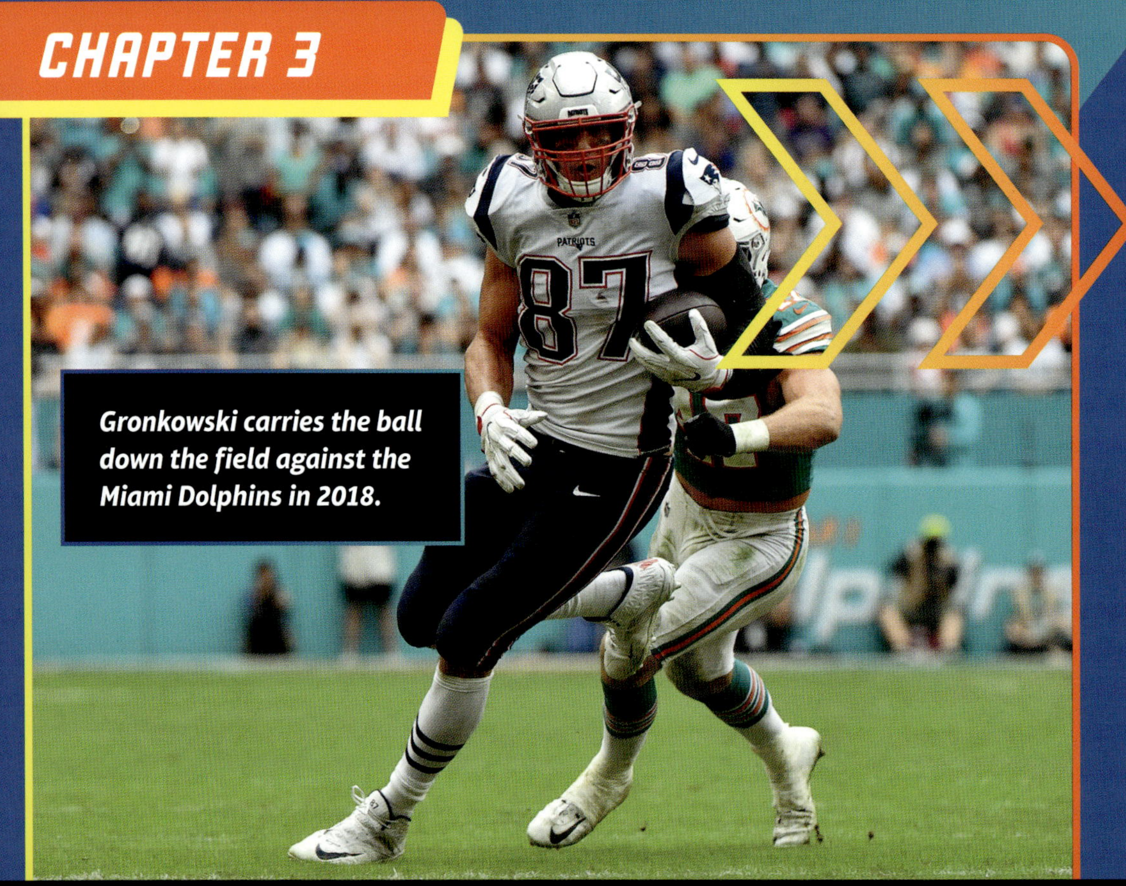

Gronkowski carries the ball down the field against the Miami Dolphins in 2018.

TERRIFIC TIGHT ENDS

Tight ends need to be able to block opponents. They also need the athletic ability to catch passes. Gronkowski and Kelce are two of the best tight ends of all time. However, they have different styles and strengths. Gronkowski was an excellent blocker. He often used his size and strength to block tackles and support his teammates. Kelce blocks less often but is a great receiver.

Both players used their unique skills to help their teams. They also benefited from playing with some of the best quarterbacks of all time. Gronkowski spent his career playing alongside Tom Brady, a three-time NFL Most Valuable Player (MVP). Kelce's success on the field took off after two-time MVP quarterback Patrick Mahomes joined the Kansas City Chiefs in 2017.

Kelce and quarterback Patrick Mahomes (left) have played together since 2017.

Gronkowski rushes to block a defender during a 2018 game against the Pittsburgh Steelers.

Gronkowski and Kelce are both record-breaking tight ends. Gronkowski held a number of league records that Kelce would later break. Gronkowski was once the fastest tight

CONSIDER THIS

Gronkowski has made many film and TV appearances. He is known for his positive, fun-loving personality. Kelce runs a popular podcast with his brother, Jason. He also brought many new fans to the NFL after he started dating singer-songwriter Taylor Swift in 2023.

end to reach 8,000 receiving yards. He hit that milestone in 120 games. In 2021, Kelce broke his record in 113 games. Later that same season, Kelce broke one of Gronkowski's records again. Kelce reached 9,000 career receiving yards in only 127 games. It had taken Gronkowski 140 games to reach this number. In Kelce's 140th game, he set the record for the fastest tight end to hit 10,000 receiving yards.

Kelce celebrates the Chiefs' 2025 AFC Championship win with girlfriend Taylor Swift.

CHAPTER 4

Gronkowski holds up the Vince Lombardi Trophy after winning the Super Bowl in 2015.

AND THE WINNER IS

So who wins this all-star smackdown? It is a tight matchup. Many people will have different opinions.

Gronkowski and Kelce have both proven their talent on the field with multiple records, awards, and titles. Gronkowski has won four Super Bowls—three with the New England

Patriots and one with the Tampa Bay Buccaneers. Kelce has won three Super Bowls, all with the Kansas City Chiefs.

Both tight ends have won many awards. They both have been on the First-Team All-Pro list four times. The First-Team All-Pro is a list that ranks the best NFL players in each position. They have also each been selected to the Pro Bowl multiple times. The Pro Bowl is an annual game featuring the league's best players. Gronkowski is a five-time Pro Bowl player, while Kelce has been selected 10 times.

Kelce celebrates his third Super Bowl win with the Kansas City Chiefs in 2024.

This is a smackdown of inches, but in the end, it goes to Travis Kelce. Kelce has more catches and more receiving yards overall. While both players have shattered many NFL records, Kelce broke many of Gronkowski's own records. But the biggest factor is Kelce's ability to stay healthy and avoid injury. And while Gronkowski is retired, Kelce is also still out there playing and racking up points. Who knows what will be next for him? He has been very dominant so far, and there's always next season!

Who do you think should have won? Think about each player's accomplishments. Consider their stats. Decide for yourself who the winner should be.

After retiring from playing, Gronkowski became a TV announcer for football games.

Kelce runs with the ball during Super Bowl 58.

SMACKDOWN BREAKDOWN

ROB GRONKOWSKI

Height: 6 feet 6 (2 m)
First-Team All-Pro: 4
Pro Bowl selections: 5
Super Bowl wins: 4

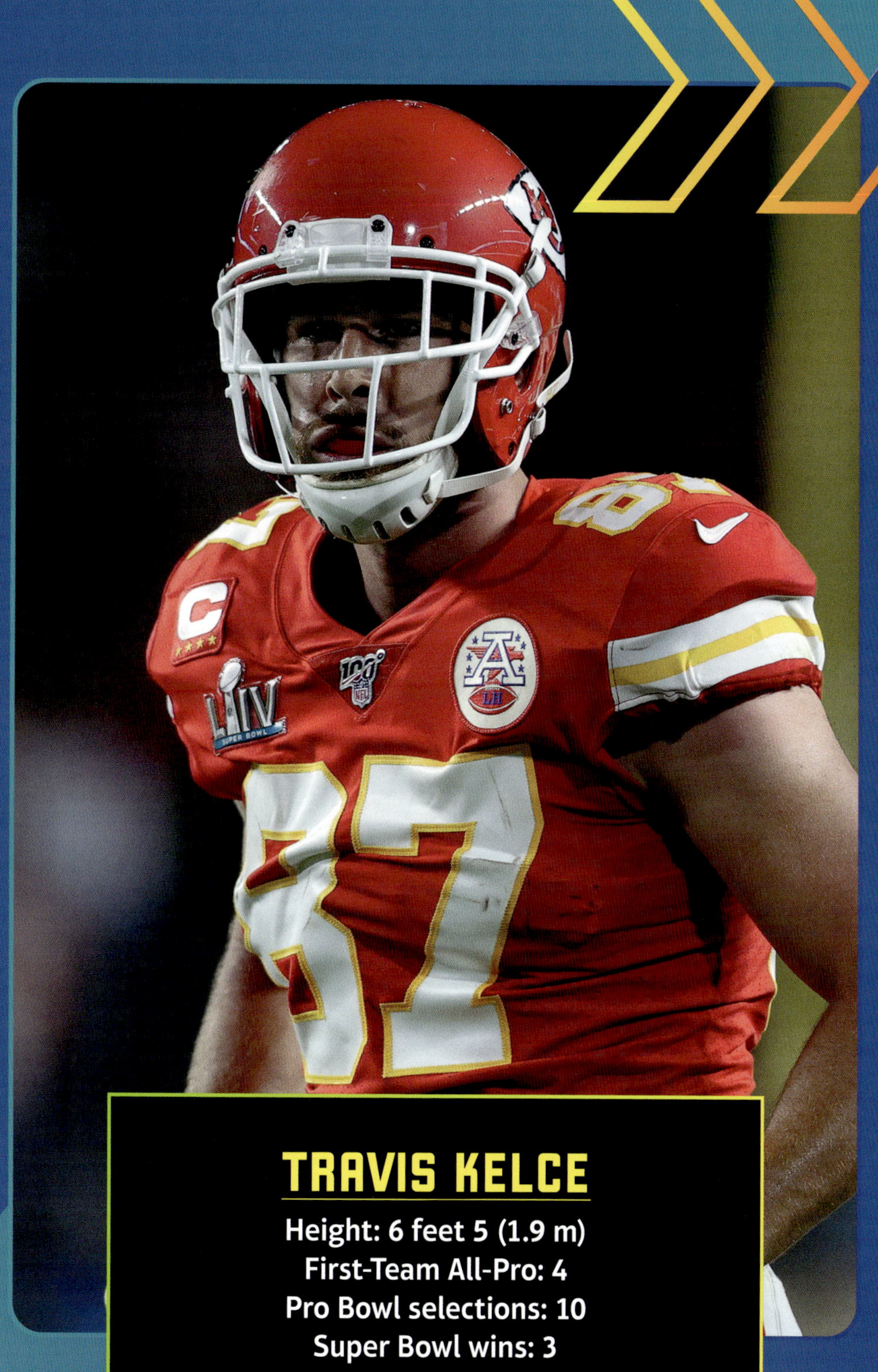

TRAVIS KELCE

Height: 6 feet 5 (1.9 m)
First-Team All-Pro: 4
Pro Bowl selections: 10
Super Bowl wins: 3

GLOSSARY

block: using the arms and body to stop a defender from tackling a teammate

Comeback Player of the Year: an award given to a player who overcomes a challenge, like a serious injury

draft: when teams take turns choosing new players

opponent: a player on the other team

playoffs: a series of games played to decide a champion

podcast: an online show where hosts discuss a specific topic

position: a player's role on their team

receiver: a player who catches a pass

rookie: a player in their first year

tight end: a player whose main job is to block and catch passes

LEARN MORE

Anderson, Josh. *G.O.A.T. Football Tight Ends*. Lerner Publications, 2024.

Britannica Kids: Kansas City Chiefs
https://kids.britannica.com/students/article/Kansas-City-Chiefs/571013

Kiddle: National Football League Facts for Kids
https://kids.kiddle.co/National_Football_League

Kiddle: Rob Gronkowski Facts for Kids
https://kids.kiddle.co/Rob_Gronkowski

Klepeis, Alicia Z. *The New England Patriots*. Bellwether Media, 2024.

Labrecque, Ellen. *Who Is Travis Kelce?* Penguin Workshop, 2024.

INDEX

PHOTO ACKNOWLEDGMENTS

Image credits: Cooper Neill/Getty Images, p. 4; Michael Reaves/Getty Images, p. 5; Tom Pennington/Getty Images, p. 6; Kevin C. Cox/Getty Images, p. 7; Louis Lopez/Cal Sport Media/Newscom, p. 8; KEVIN P. CASEY/Icon SMI 266/ Newscom, p. 9; Andy Lyons/Getty Images, p. 10; Streeter Lecka/Getty Images, p. 11; Orlin Wagner/ASSOCIATED PRESS, p. 12; Kevin Mazur/WireImage/Getty Images, p. 13; Tom Hauck/Getty Images, p. 14; Jonathan Daniel/Getty Images, p. 15; Mike Ehrmann/Getty Images, p. 16; Ryan Kang/Getty Images, p. 17; Focus on Sport/Getty Images, p. 18; Cooper Neill/Getty Images, p. 19; Mark Brown/Getty Images, p. 20; Jamie Squire/Getty Images, p. 21; Joe Sargent/ Getty Images, p. 22; Jamie Squire/Getty Images, p. 23; Christian Petersen/ Getty Images, p. 24; Michael Owens/Getty Images, p. 25; Gregory Shamus/ Getty Images, p. 26; Michael Owens/Getty Images, p. 27; Michael Reaves/Getty Images, p. 28; Tom Pennington/Getty Images, p. 29.

Cover: David Smith/Cal Sport Media/Newscom; Icon Sportswire/Newscom.